Something About the Way

Something About the Way

Poems by

Peter Waldor

Cover design by Shay Culligan

ISBN: 978-1-952326-55-4

Kelsay Books
502 South 1040 East, A-119
American Fork, Utah, 84003

for Lisa Allee

Acknowledgments

The American Poetry Review: "Wonder Bread"

The Courtship of Winds: "Mindfulness #1," "In the Golden Period"

34th Parallel Magazine: "Two Stray Dogs"

Delmarva Review: "Breach," "Crazy (E) Motion"

Chiron: "Cliché"

Blue Moon: "Cheat Sheet"

Bitchin' Kitsch: "I Love How (your friend used)"

Fungi Magazine: "I Love How (gently you reach)"

Deep Overstock: "Envelope"

2River: "Doing the Dishes," "Magic Trowel"

BlazeVOX: "Cayenne," "Who Am I Really?"

Better Than Starbucks: "Instructions for Lovers"

The Big Windows: "Pendant"

Books by Peter Waldor

Door to a Noisy Room

The Wilderness Poetry of Wu Xing

Who Touches Everything

The Unattended Harp

State of the Union

Gate Posts with No Gate

Nice Dumpling

Owl Gulch Elegies

Contents

II.

III.

"Pin Pricks of Eternity"—William Blake

Two Stray Dogs

It's rare in dreams
that the next night
you can pick up
the story where you
left off the night before
but one time I found
a black dog then
a night later
the dog was in
my old home
I found a number
on its collar but I
didn't get a dial tone
It's even rarer
to wake up one day
next to a beloved
and a few days later
wake up next to
the same beloved
but oh my god
here you are
I will not look
in your locket
to find a number
Stay lost with me
Two stray dogs

I.

Tarantula Migration

A long time ago
before your family
left the garden
of nakedness
you and your sons
walked naked
from your pond
and at your feet found
a tarantula migration,
at least twenty of them.
They seemed to walk in twos.
Your boys were not afraid,
they had already learned
how to handle
the furry beasts
and you would let them,
though that day
you all just watched,
the warmth from
the red rocks passing
through your bare feet
all the way out
the ends of your hair
like sparks.
Many years later
the two of us walk naked
from the same water,
you swam across
but I could only jump in.
Was it hard to be
there with me
and your memories?

So many dragon flies
and their miracles
of flight and hovering,
better at that than the
humming bird or even
a person levitating
in a lucid dream,
though of course,
in love all comparisons
are odious.

Bed

You built your bed tall
so it won't be swamped
by stormy dreams,
but to get down
one must be a child
jumping off a jungle gym,
especially at night when
I can't see and must jump
blind from the mortised
scrap oak into everything
that doesn't matter.

Doing the Dishes

Your plates are all mismatched
as if you have one from
every kiln on earth
like Noah collecting animals
They are all old so even
the ugly ones are beautiful
like the rusty knife you use
while the box of tempered
German blades stays sealed
On one plate your grandmother
painted a trout
and though you love it more
than any object you let it
take its place on the table
Accidents don't worry you
just this darkening world
so you cook for as many
people as you can
letting them stay late
talking and laughing
and you let me
do the dishes so I
can skip the dancing
when it inevitably begins

I Love How

I remembered the names
of your children the first time you told me
and I can't remember the names of your old lovers
no matter how hard I try,
but I do remember how carefully
you place back displaced moss
and the way you chop peppers like an antique clock
and your glass petaled earrings
on the sill of your bathroom window,
the sill you hammered in with three strokes on each nail,
beginning middle end,
and the way you notice and praise things.
I wanted to touch one of those earrings
but the law protects wildflowers,
so I am left to dream of you sliding
the pedestrian post out from
your lobe that is smooth as sand
just cleared by a falling wave.
Can you really be that place?
Endless as any place I can imagine.

The Curse Goes

May you live in interesting times.
You make our times doubly interesting
so that makes me twice cursed
walking all night in the desert
waiting for your midwife shift
to end at the Fort Defiance clinic.
I know how you join the elaborate
rituals to pray for a quiet night
of naps and chatting in the call room
but you secretly hope to be busy
catching babies, trying to make
that time between taking the baby
from between the mother's legs
to placing it on her breasts
no time at all.

Your Sighs

It's about time I compared your sighs
to a distant idling engine...
say a chainsaw in the forest.
The lumberjack has had a heart attack
and the idling motor sputters along,
its sigh only coming
when the breeze is just right,
the old growth
spared for a while,
long enough for us to unroll
our tarp over the needles
and lie down and look up
before we close our eyes.
But you have begged me
to make the lumberjack just tired
with no heart disease,
so now I am not sure how to afflict him.

Breath

Your sleeping breath
on my arm,
the inhalation
undetectable but
the exhalation
puffing like an
old locomotive,
bending my arm hairs
with each breath.
We all want to sleep
soundly but how
lucky I am to be
the one awake
listening.

Wonder Bread and Speaking of Detachment

In the morning when your hips go round on me
they don't turn in a perfect circle like a giant
mixer at the Wonder Bread factory.
There is something broken in your circle

and the break differs with each turn.
I can't stop thinking of it.
Speaking of bread and detachment,
you debated whether to throw away

your own mixing bowl rather than
glue it together a second time.
On one hand, throwing it away
would symbolize detachment,

but how beautiful the glued cracks.
You realize the worst
of all attachments
is that to detachment.

Lichen

I love how you turn
your hat brim backwards
like a young gangsta
so your head can rest
on a boulder tilted just
off vertical, covered
by a crazy quilt of lichens.
You are at peace
for a long time and the
lichen is at peace with you,
practicing its work
as the great rock destroyer.

Beets

That time between the time
I knew I loved you and
when I told you so was the few weeks
it took you to dig up your beets
and place them in the fermentation
jars and wait for the sugars to drench
the softening tubers and the color
to darken to deep burgundy.
But why not when you dug them up?
With your dirty hands, the fine
hairs hanging from the tuber.
Why wait to say what had to be said?

Two Watershed Moments

Deep in a religious text
a watershed moment.
One group dips their heads in to drink.
The other uses their hands as a cup.
This is where man separates from beast,
and tonight at El Moro Tavern in Durango
in the chaos of Saturday night
late stage capitalist abundance
you dip your head to your plate
and lick the sauce,
taking your time and mostly oblivious
to the entertainment you provide and oblivious
to this watershed moment where we
learn to be primitive again.

Jumping In

Pigs whistling, crickets gasp,
a fat lady sighs after her song,
hinges creak, and one tree falls,
alone in the forest, screaming,
without a friend, a lover,
but your friend jumps in
a mostly frozen river
without a sound and you
notice some lichen on
an interior wall and spray it
after you wind your mother's clocks.
The particles of mist shoot out
like last ships leaving earth
in search of another home.

The Lama's Braid

Good thing I didn't wash
in a while for I touched
some pine sap and smell it
on my fingers along
with some manchego
and your sacred juice,
the three smells braided
like a Lama's hair
swinging behind him
as he crosses India
looking for the sacred river
that sprang up where
the enlightened one's arrow
fell to earth. The Lama
doesn't think he is
better than anyone,
but I can't help it
because of our love.

Clothes

You've got a pile of clothes
in your attic room.
I love seeing arms or waists
sticking out like a glove
from a closed glove compartment.
You have cut the necks
wider in your boys'
old shirts and one pair of pants
has a row of green sequins.
It's a small pile
but a theatre troupe could
put on a production
with them, especially
if they were from
Dharamsala India.
Now that I have seen you
wear all of them
I can't wait to see you
wear them again
like watching a great
movie over and over,
only this time I am sitting
next to you and we have
time to talk afterwards.

There Is Something Amazing About the Way

while walking you say offhand
wise things to me and now that
you love me and told me so and you
have offered to cancel the three to five day
river trip with your old partner
I don't feel the torture of the other
with his hammered copper bracelet.
You see I am completely unadorned.

Bite

In a fit of weakness
I bite you, your thigh,
and we wait quietly
the few moments
for the bruise to surface,
like invisible ink
after the lemon
tincture was sprinkled
on the blank page.
You weren't angry,
you weren't perplexed,
but I could tell
you weren't happy
and I hoped this
would be one of
those rare bites
that left no mark.

I love how

gently you reach
your two largest fingers
of your left hand
under mushroom caps
to feel if they are gilled,
gently as a seamstress
feeling under a hem
or a midwife palpating
a cervix, so the delicate
nether region will not
be disturbed.

Pendant

One time your pendant,
ammonite in blue resin,
fell into my mouth
and I let it stay
a moment too long.
I was like one
about to swallow
a secret page
from the resistance
so it won't fall
into the wrong hands.

Magic Trowel

Your hand
briefly
on my hand,
teaching me
the trowel,
to leave
no trace of the
instrument,
and to angle
everything slightly
so liquids won't pool.
I wonder if you'll
notice the faint
crescent moon I left.
Will it bother you?
It's waxing,
always.

I Love How

your friend used the word
"demarcation" in casual conversation
first time in the history of the word
and then she told us
how to identify currants
and make currant pancakes
in the wilderness
and though you were friends
for decades and talked
about everything under the sun
you were rapt

Cayenne

A long time ago, in a moment
of desperation, you placed a poultice
of cayenne pepper over your clogged duct.

Thirty years later, I try every
trick I can with the same breast.
Sometimes we are perpendicular

like one hand at twelve and one at nine.
Sometimes we kiss and don't make love
and sometimes we make love

and don't kiss and sometimes
we kiss and make love—
you taught me this

last way is not always best.
In pain, you forgot to wipe away
the cayenne before nursing again.

That baby is near middle age now,
loves spicy food more than anything
and lives pretty close to home.

Who Am I Really?

With great subtle fanfare,
next to the trail,
I moved a rock off a flower,
a hare bell, which sprang back.
I didn't look to see if you noticed
because I wanted you to think
it was all a natural part of me.
I repeated the maneuver
several times, each time I'd
place the rock on another rock
just off the trail, so it wouldn't be
kicked onto another flower,
and I positioned it so any lichens
on either rock wouldn't be covered.
Feeling guilty about my designs,
I thought I should give you a fuller
picture of me so I told you about
my book of horror movie sketches,
full of slow dismemberments,
unanesthetized surgeries and all
manner of rusty piercings.
You just shrugged off the horrors,
even telling me your daughter,
with her partner, slide hooks
through their flesh,
at least a dozen and then they
thread the hooks and hoist
each other into the air.
She is Navajo and there is
a similar Lakota practice.
She lives happily in the suburbs
and they do their suspensions
with humor, concentration and tenderness.

Barbed Arrow

There is a story that when
the Buddha won an archery contest,
where his arrow landed,
a river of enlightenment
sprung from the earth.
My love found an arrow
deep in the forest, not tipped
but barbed with four cross blades.
I thought she thought it was
unsightly, so she tucked it into
her pack, but she did so because
she worried an animal might cut
itself walking through the forest.
Unfortunately she tumbled
in the snow and the arrow
fell out, perhaps even worse now
for it is no longer lodged
in the earth. How hard it is
to remove evil. Must it stay
like a last vile of virus
frozen in a science lab?
For all that, the arrow was
at least carried closer
to the edge of the forest
where someone else may
find it and take it to a place
where it won't stick out.

I love How

you call me Ishmael as if
it really is my name
and you've used it for decades.
I love how your thighs open
like an old book and I
am the preacher placing
his fingers in the dark groove
where pages begin and end.
You are the only one
who has ever used my name.

Cheat Sheet

It's embarrassing how little
I know and how much you do.
It's been a string of miracles
you haven't seen me sneaking
a look at my tiny cheat sheets;
embarrassing how little I have
lived and how much you have.
If only I had a perfect memory
to remember everything you say,
but I do remember how tonight's
light frost will turn the starches
in your apples to sugars.

Experiment

After a morning
in each other's arms
celebrating conventional
lovemaking you
rolled away
then turned back
and said "you know
you can experiment
with me," and with
all the troubles in
the world I can only
think of those words.

II.

I Love How

when I tell you
my brave thoughtful
musings about your
old lovers all you
do is laugh
You are like the
sage on top
of the mountain
when the acolyte
clambers up
and asks what is
the meaning of life
and the sage holds
her stomach
and laughs heartily
The sage didn't
think the acolyte
was funny
but I pray
you think
I am

One Thing

It would be one thing
if you loved me
and then loved others
because you were afraid
of your love for me
and it would be
another thing
if you loved me
and then loved others
simply because
you loved others
or is there even
one thing
or another
or is it all
simply love

Tying Your Shoe Laces

It's always good
to dream of one lover
when with another lover.
It's like dreaming of your right
lace while I tie your left.
I kneel before you,
and leave the laces
in loose knots,
two droopy butterflies
hovering off the ground
where no one looks.

I Love How

1.

I love how our chests
fit like two pine planks
at Four Corners Lumber,
the pile just off vertical.
Our boards
are in the middle,
at least half a dozen
on either side
pressing our backs.

2.

Saying I love you
is like saying everything
that doesn't matter
and then afterwards
saying everything
that needs to be said.
It could take what's left
of a lifetime.

3.

Anything you could
ever do to yourself
would be gilding
the lily, but I love
how you gild,
the way you pull out
a child's splinter,

gently, of course,
while telling a story
about something
unrelated.

4.

I love how you ask for
definitions of words
you don't know.
I am one who pretends
to know everything.

5.

I want to give you
more pleasure than you give me
and you want to give me
more pleasure than I give you,
like two warring countries
who both want peace
but neither negotiates.

6.

Falling in love is like falling
out of love, one just slides
one's hand into the reversed
sleeve and pulls it out.

7.

Peaches the size
of ping pong balls
next to a tall glass
with an inch of water.
Two pensioners wake up,
with no obligations
and fall back to sleep.

8.

I love how you don't mind
I forgot the different
varieties of Buddhism.

9.

You take care of me,
no matter what.

10.

I Love how
you don't use
napkins or tissues
but you do use
three squares
of toilet paper,

leaving the radicals
to collect corn lillies
for their necessities.

11.

Awake but frozen
for two hours because
your left hand has fallen
to rest on my thigh.

12.

How shameless
my loose pants
with no belt
and pockets empty,
trying to give you
easy access.

13.

We live separately
and when we part
I drink from your cup,
and I learned,
in your quiet home,
you drink from mine.

14.

Four small peach pits
at the edge of a narrow
table and some pants
tied in a knot below.

15.

The veining
in the dragonfly wing
divides the great
surface into hundreds
of small spaces,
like rural counties
on a map where
everyone knows
each other's name.

16.

You taught me it's ok
to leave salad out
all night and eat
it for breakfast.

17.

So my parents won't
be lucky enough to fall
in love with you
but my children will.

18.

One pine nut left
on a pine slab.
Last night.

19.

A chop saw
blocks the way
to your room.
The saw dust grows
ever fainter away
from the blade.

20.

I love to slide my hand
down your smooth
railing in the morning—

the one I can't stay
upright without,
a memory of you fixing
it onto the balusters before
you sanded and rubbed
the oil with your soft rag.

21.

So much was separating us,
then, at the same time,
we threw the covers off.

22.

I love to wipe my face in your dirty towel.

23.

Five wild iris seed pods
in a cup on your window sill.
You combed the meadow
all summer and waited
to go back until they were
shriveled, ready.

24.

To be entered or to enter. What's the difference?

25.

Heel resting in buttocks.
A stirrup.

26.

Falling in love is like going out of business.
No one comes to the sale even though
everything is marked down to nothing.
It's just us loading the perfectly good stuff
to take home because neither of us
can bare to take it to the dump.

27.

My forearm weighted
against your dark area
and my palm spread underneath
as if waiting for a bird.

28.

Two large stone hearts at your door
like childhood friends who meet
again by accident in old age.
It must have taken two people
to carry each heart,
and so far it looks like the lichens
have survived the transit.

29.

Perhaps I am a lost voice
or perhaps like everyone else
I just think I am a lost voice.
You are wise enough not
to say there is no difference.

30.

If there must be others
and you must mention them,
curse and spit the way
my grandmother
Gertrude would,
to avoid the evil eye,
three spits with
no phlegm.

31.

What a shame I told you
how I stole my butter knife
from the Alhambra Palace Hotel
forty years ago, a shame
I didn't just butter your toast
with butter from the
Kalona Amish Organic Coop
and make you a hot honey
lemon ginger tea, quietly.

32.

I've seen you swing planks
onto saw horses and lower
your maul through green wood
so I knew your strength
before you held me
and I wasn't frightened.

33.

The whole idea of the muse
disgusts me, but who are you
who has listened patiently,
smiled and even asked me
to repeat things?
You would put any
goddamn muse to shame!

34.

I love how you leave the key
in your front door
when you leave. You only
lock it because you worry
about the wind blowing it open.
You love the wind
and the wind loves you
but you don't want your
lover rummaging
without you.

Nina Cassian

Since we just met and were falling in love
my brother asked if I told you
the Nina Cassian lines—*I promise*
to make you so alive the sound of
dust falling on furniture will deafen you,
but what an insult to resort to cheap tricks
with you...if anything, when we kiss,
I place my hands over your ears
because the dust was deafening for you
long before we met.

Why Not Why Not?

Why not just love me
and leave the loving
others to me?
I could tell you stories
in a whisper under
the slow burning
chakra candle?
Why not become
friends with my other
lovers, even cook
and look after them?
You alone
can heal them.

Lubrication

Why not let your spit
spill onto me and keep
the precious oil
in the cabinet?

III.

Cliché

Who doesn't dream
of restoring the abandoned
collapsing house
set way back off
the county road?
Dream of walking in
with a pail in each hand,
the first tools
for the project?
All of us.
But I know you
who built your house
mostly with your own hands
and in fourteen months
got a temporary certificate
of occupancy.
You aren't even a carpenter
or any kind of contractor.
Your last project, to spread
seed and manure
for the meadow which
will outlast any house.
I don't know how to tell you
I love you most drenched
in sweat, in your torn, stained,
dirty work pants and shirt,
right after you pull off
your leather gloves
and lock your hands
behind my back.

I Love How

you don't mind
I haven't done psychotherapy,
meditation, yoga or a finely orchestrated
long-term naturopathic regime,
but that I let my childhood drip
like blood from an exacto knife
stuck in my thigh instead,
dripping on your new
cherry floors before they
have been sealed,
and to make matters worse I drag the leg,
making a scraping sound,
so you think the floors
are being scratched every
time I move.

The Dragonfly Effect

Your legs athwart me and on
that bone that protrudes from
your ankle for no evolutionary advantage,
a dragonfly has landed.
They are the most skitterish of creatures
but this one is comfortable
resting on that spot and though
humans may be the second most skitterish
of creatures you let it rest. Most people
find them frightening but you
think it's mysteriously beautiful.
So here you are with your legs
athwart me, both you and the dragon
have fallen asleep. Perhaps you are
both awake in your dreams and are
true equals that can ask each other
questions in dire circumstances.

What Is It That You Are Dipped In?

That golden, brownish, red rock
color, you glow so bright
it keeps me awake. You are
one of those fiery goddesses
in a rolled cloth travel painting.
At the Super 8 Motel I take down
the Grand Canyon photo with
the Vishnu schist and hang
your painting on the tack.
I know I should leave it
for the next guest but they will
have to find another way
to change their life.

With the Terrible History

of the sexes it could be dangerous
talking about a woman's cooking
but I love how with almost no
provisions you can make almost
anything, even if I am at your back
trying my best to distract you.
No drama, just the best eggplant
involtini ever created,
the chevre tucked in like a magician's
scarf in his closed fist.

Giant Black Pot

One day a giant black pot
with gray flecks and some
kind of lattice inside.
Another day the pot
is gone and there are
eight wide jars
of peaches as if the glass
just came from
the glass blower and the
tin lid from the long-
suffering tin smith
and the peaches from
that mythological garden
that was actually the most
real place on earth.
Who knows what lucky
cupboards they have
been placed into,
so on that darkest day,
when a sadness for the ages
plagues a lonely man
who can't seem to warm up
your peaches will save him.

The Way You Dress

as if Paquin the Parisian
developed a line of dirty
old work jeans and
cotton shirts infused
with saw dust and
chain saw oil.
The couture must
have worked in secret
for years to balance
all the elements.
It's hard to imagine
you in your medical
fatigues but I dream
of stripping them off
to discover what is
beneath after one
of your long nights
of welcoming babies.
I imagine you'd have
the energy to take
your hands
that held newborns,
the left hand on the
right side, fingers spread
down from the soft
part of the skull
to the shoulders,
and the right hand
around and over
the left side,
fingers spread from
the bottom of the back
across the buttocks
to the top of the thighs,

as you pass
the baby to the mother
who hardly knew
she was home to
those two great
calderas of milk.
You who, unlike
the others, make
inquiries after
mother and child
go home and would
help until the baby
was an old woman,
if the wheels of
time didn't stop you.
Oh my, I forgot what
I was talking about,
your amazing hands,
a long night
is over and one hand
is on my shoulder
and the other
on my chest.

I Love How

you talked about the beetle killed
clapboards on your cabin,
pointing out the worm tracks,
the wide even seams
one could wedge a folded note in,
the sawmill marks which are
like fingerprints,
their pungent odors before
and after the sealer,
and their embarrassing
yellowness the local
authorities will object to
and so although you question
all authority, local,
spiritual, even the
United Nations,
you are already
mixing a light stain.

I Could See What Was Happening

I don't know whether
it was your hand
seeking me out
behind you or my
getting close to you
but you found me and I could
quickly feel what was happening
and I didn't want you to think
I was that easy
so first I thought of
that terrible first day of kindergarten,
that didn't work,
then I dreamed of my friend
Frank Farro eating grass
in Siberia for a whole year,
that didn't work,
then that day when,
by mistake, I walked into
an autopsy room precisely
when they were working
on the groin,
that didn't work,
so you see, with you,
I am the easiest person
in the world.

Sex

It's easier to talk in the wilderness,
so above tree line, on Yellow Mountain,
we talked about it, finally, we even found
a dusty spot in the scree and drew with
our fingers—an arrow for the tongue,
two crescents for our bodies,
one behind the other and the hand-lines
not so different from the ridge we were on,
until it was all chaos, there were so many ideas
and then you smoothed it out with your
left hand like a good student called up
to the front for the honor of erasing
the blackboard which turned from black
to gray with the debris of all the old symbols.

In Our First Conversation

In our first conversation
you said you wanted to sleep out
on top of a mountain and I worried
it meant you were only interested
in friendship for who in their
right mind would so quickly suggest
an activity like that if they had
romantic intentions?

Shaolin

I finally became a Shaolin monk
walking down your rice paper stairs
without leaving a trace or sound.
I knew I passed the test when
my blind master, who was waiting
at the bottom, wasn't only smiling,
he was laughing.
So I am ready to sling my bedroll
over one shoulder and go
into the wilderness and when
I return I will climb the same stairs,
feet pointing out, slowly starting
the footfall with the toes.
I can make it all the way
and you will still be asleep.

Lover and Beloved

They say there is always a lover and a beloved,
just as an angry assistant manager must
rest his elbow on the market counter
while telling the squatting clerk
to move the Kalamata olives
a half-inch closer to the roasted peppers.
But I'd like to think of us as two blind mice,
our great streaming whiskers
brushing each other as we grope along.
It's all organic, the clerk thinks,
so what's the difference?

In the Golden Period

Today at the Zen center
in Po Chu San my eyes
were too often open in
the meditation circle,
but how delightful
to sit quietly in
a room with others.
I looked at your
legs folded perfectly
as oiled shears,
and up to the great
cliff where Du Fu
once camped
in the golden period.
The noisy river filled
the room and later
you told me your vision—
you got a Koch brother's
address from your son
and sent a letter that arrived
at just the right moment
to convince them to stop
destroying the earth.
When my eyes were closed,
just as when open,
my vision was only of you.
Does this make me
the lover and you the beloved?

Mindfulness #1

As my hand travels just above you
my broken leather watch strap
drags across your chest,
like a muffler hanging off
a Chevelle on Route 280.
At high speed the metal
and concrete spark in the
car's dark undercarriage
and the driver in the car behind
first curses the noise and then
notices the sparks and thinks
of them as catching in a feathery
ball of kindling deep
in the forest of mind.

Mindfulness #2

The Zen master, far along
in her practice, finally
placed all her quartz
and crystals in a cardboard
box and left it on the curb
for recycling, not sure
the truck would take the box.
A girl noticed it on her way
home from school and hoisted
it on her shoulder and later
that day, in her room,
hung the crystals creating
a concatenation of dusk rainbows,
and she arrayed the quartz
on her two window sills.
Once, a crystal rainbow
gleamed out and a bird
that couldn't see the glass
and would have crashed,
saw the rainbow, and pulled back.

Envelope

You find a long dried
bouquet of wild daisies
and asters, yellow daisies,
purple asters, the daisy
petals folded back
like a comet's tail.
The aster petals are gone
and you pinch
the globe of seeds
and drop them into
an envelope never to
hold a check or love letter,
separating the seeds
between thumb and pointer
with the same gentle action
as pinching salt on a delicacy.
There is a barren hillside
and though it's late
in autumn you say it's not
too late, or at least they can
rest there until spring.

Not Nearly Long Enough!

The lord made the groin areas
of the man and woman
so radically different
in their extreme concavities
and convexities,
but how mysteriously
similar are the nipples!
To the best of my knowledge
the male nipple was never
used for milk.
Why are they there,
like two marks on a wall where
an old master painting once hung?
How logical for the woman's nipples
to be packed with their various
sensory mechanisms for pleasure.
How logical the male obsession
with women's nipples and women's
neglect of male nipples,
but you have changed the history
of humanity, sliding your hand
up my shirt cautiously as a child
reaching under a couch for a
lost dart, palms and fingers
dwell on the two rises.
Could there be
a slight hardening?
What a long time you spent
and not nearly long enough!
Like a cautious young lover
who felt up her friend's shirt
for the first time you did not
strip my shirt off and attack
first with lips, then tongue,

then teeth, crossing back and forth
over the unguarded border
between pain and pleasure.
That would happen soon enough.

Crazy (E) Motion

I found an unwrapped candy
under a hotel bed,
translucent, gelatinous,
pressed from a locomotive mold.
How delightful "loco"
begins locomotive.
Crazy motion!
Whereas I always welcome
unbidden sweetness, this is
Boulder, Colorado, I am
afraid the candy is infused
with tetrahydrocannabinol
and I don't want to cloud
my love for you. I am a child
who just learned the alphabet.
I want to keep the glittering
letters lined up.
I don't even want to
string them into words.

Degenerate Midwives

I'd like to say I am my beloved's
and she is mine as it says in the
bible but the truth is she belongs
to no one and neither do I.
She formed a group called
The Degenerate Midwives.
They just traveled to a rural
hospital in India to offer help.
Why "degenerate?" I think
because they don't drink.
They just meditate and walk
at night without lights.

Male, Female, Other

I only love half the world
and you love the whole thing,
like someone who stays up
all night and all day,
and not only because
the Fort Defiance Clinic
has you on the midnight
midwife shift; it could
also be dancing, a séance,
canning tomatoes,
not putting a book down,
or talking to your mother,
and you don't nap or
drink coffee.

Breach

On the Lost Coast a Cessna
flew you in with supplies
to cook for a Buddhist retreat
and the pilot circled back
because he saw swirling waters,
the trace of whales.
Maybe we'll get lucky
and they'll breach, he said,
and they breached.
Then you stirred your bolete, barley
rosemary, soup with your spoon
carved from a kumbuk tree
blown down during a hurricane
in Sri Lanka 57 years ago.
What I would like to know,
for those who walked away
from that wild place
with the light step of transformation,
was it the meditation or your cooking?
When you stirred,
an echo of the swirling.

Gardening

My love, like her father before her,
gardens naked, she presses seeds
in those wafer containers.
She has scarified the tomato seeds
and places all the containers
along her south facing windows
while the spring snows still
wrap around the house.
In one of the old pots she finds
a preying mantis chrysalis,
it's dusty and cavernous
and she carries the container
out to the barn and places it
in a quiet corner, so there
is a chance it can enter
this world peacefully.
I water for her and she is
anxious I'll pour in too much
and wash the seeds away.
Her elbows and calves
are covered with potting soil.
She is both one giant seed
and one giant plant that has
forgotten its seed long ago.
She has had a life full
of love and loss and I would
like to surprise her from behind,
spin her around and pin
her hands over her head,
but, I just water, carefully.

Later I tell her about my desire
and she responds the way
she did when I told her
about my crimes, she just
laughed, I don't know why.

Retired Watch Maker

How can it be that my love and I
can kiss passionately and both
fall asleep during the kiss?
Minutes later we wake and the same
thing happens, happens many times
as if night after night we start a great book
and fall asleep during the first paragraph,
so often we learn those few words by heart.
It doesn't mean our passion is gone.
Just the opposite, we have found
that secret place all lovers search for,
it could be an island off the charts
or an abandoned building in the city,
that quiet place where time both stops
and could give us whiplash if we don't hold on,
that place where we appear in each other's dreams,
this morning I blew a ram's horn in my love's dream
and in mine she is building a magic box,
patient as a retired watch maker.
How lucky to fall asleep while we kiss
and to wake up laughing.

Silver

On the black
soapstone a long
silver hair,
if it were still
a black hair
it would be invisible,
but the silver is
a kind of light,
as if the hair was
part of a body
that had learned
to give off light,
it didn't come
naturally or easily,
like for those
sea creatures that
glow in the dark,
it came after
a long time,
and the light itself
is like a dim lantern
that lets us see
a bit further but
doesn't ruin our eyes
from seeing the subtle
shades of night.

Instructions for Lovers

Touch as gently
as you can
as if you were
picking up one
sesame seed
and your fingers
glanced against
the floor boards
and then
and only then

About the Author

Peter Waldor is the author of nine books of poetry, including *Who Touches Everything,* which won the National Jewish Book Award. His poetry has appeared widely in magazines. He lives in Trout Lake, Colorado.